W9-BNS-415

Your

Travel

Guide to

ANCIENT
ROME

Your Travel Guide to

ANCIENT ROME

Rita J. Markel

LERNER PUBLICATIONS COMPANY • MINNEAPOLIS

To David

Lerner Publications Company
A division of Lerner Publishing Group
241 First Avenue North
Minneapolis, MN 55401 U.S.A.

Website address: www.lernerbooks.com

Library of Congress Cataloging-in-Publication Data

Markel, Rita J.
    Your travel guide to ancient Rome / by Rita J. Markel.
        p.   cm. — (Passport to history)
    Includes bibliographical references and index.
    ISBN: 0–8225–3071–6 (lib. bdg. : alk. paper)
    1. Rome—Guidebooks—Juvenile literature. 2. Rome—Civilization—Juvenile
literature. 3. Rome—Social life and customs—Juvenile literature. I. Title.
II. Passport to history
(Minneapolis, Minn.)
DG78.M367 2004
937—dc21   2003003561

Manufactured in the United States of America
1 2 3 4 5 6 – JR – 09 08 07 06 05 04

CONTENTS

INTRODUCTION

GETTING STARTED

Welcome to Passport to History. You will be traveling through time and space to ancient Rome between the years 27 B.C. and A.D. 180. This handy guide will help you every step of the way, answering questions such as:

- ➤ **What will I see?**
- ➤ **How do I get around?**
- ➤ **How should I dress?**
- ➤ **The restrooms are *where?***

Remember, you are going back in time to an ancient culture. Almost everything you'd use on an ordinary trip didn't exist during this period. So leave your camera at home—there was no photography back then. No e-mail, no instant messaging. You won't find any ATMs, either. Ancient Rome may seem a little strange at first, but you'll be okay. Just do what the Romans do. Well, maybe not *everything* the Romans do.

The garden courtyard of a villa (large home) in Pompeii, an ancient Roman city on the southeastern coast of the Italian Peninsula

NOTE TO THE TRAVELER

A lot of the information in this guidebook comes from the best source you can get: the people who actually lived in the days of ancient Rome. The Romans left many letters, poems, plays, speeches, and histories that tell us how they lived and what they believed. They also left technical books, government papers, and legal documents. These writings tell us what they knew about such things as medicine, science, geography, architecture, and city planning.

THE ROMAN
EMPIRE AT ITS LARGEST
A.D.118

BRITISH
ISLES

EUROPE

Rhine River

N

Danube River

BLACK SEA

Tiber
R.

ADRIATIC SEA

ITALY

Rome
Ostia

Mt.
Vesuvius

Pompeii

Brundisium

GREECE

MIDDLE
EAST

Carthage

Athens

MEDITERRANEAN SEA

Miles

0   200   400

0   200   400   600

Kilometers

Jerusalem

EGYPT

NORTH AFRICA

Nile River

Other objects give us clues about life in ancient Rome, too. Archaeologists study Roman artifacts and the remains of the many roads, aqueducts (structures to carry water into cities), and other useful things the
Romans built across the vast territory of their empire. Art historians ex-
amine Roman works of art, including monuments, sculptures, frescoes,
and mosaics, to tell us more about these ancient people. Experts are still
studying the empire. New studies and archaeological digs—some of

them underwater!—continue to give us more information. You may find new things, too, as you travel back through time. If you do, record them carefully. Everyone wants to learn more about the ancient Romans.

WHY VISIT ANCIENT ROME?

Let's put it this way. When a small village grows into one of the greatest empires in history, it's worth a visit. After taking control of what became Italy, Rome gradually gained power over the Mediterranean Sea and all the lands that bordered it. This region was home to such great cities as Athens, Carthage, and Jerusalem. At its peak, the Roman Empire reached north to the British Isles and east to the Persian Gulf. Millions of people of different cultures and languages were united under the Roman system of law and government.

Even after the empire's decline and eventual fall in A.D. 476, the Romans continued to influence many other people and cultures, including our own. The legal and political systems of many modern European, South American, and North American countries were based on those of

Back TO THE FUTURE

Languages such as French, Spanish, and Italian are called Romance languages. This is not because they're spoken by people in love. It's because they are based on the official language of the Romans: Latin. Even English, which is not a Romance language, has lots of words that come from Latin.

the Romans. Roman architecture and engineering were studied and imitated long after the empire was gone. Except for a few side trips, this guide concentrates on a period known as the Pax Romana (27 B.C.–A.D. 180), which begins with the reign of Augustus, the first official Roman emperor.

Pax Romana is Latin for "Roman Peace." Don't be fooled by the term. An empire as big and varied as Rome's is never really at peace. A military battle is almost always going on somewhere. Since lots of people have their own ideas on who should lead the empire, political battles take place, too—some resulting in takeover plots, murder, rebellion, and even civil war. It might be more accurate to call this period "The Closest Thing to Peace Those Romans Were Ever Gonna See." Still, it is the first time in history that so many people of different cultures live together in relative stability under one government for such a long time. The Pax Romana is the empire at its best.

Hot Hint

One reason that the Roman Empire lasted as long as it did was that the emperors gradually granted citizenship to the people they had conquered. In the first and second centuries A.D., non-Romans actually gained considerable power in the Roman government.

THE BASICS

A Roman procession crosses a sturdy Roman bridge. The emperor Tiberius finished constructing the bridge in A.D. 21. Its pillars unite in a single, stable foundation on the riverbed, and it is still in use in modern Italy.

LOCATION LOWDOWN

The Romans had an advantage from the very start. They built their city in a great location. In ancient times, this meant that they could defend themselves from attack. Rome was formed when the folks living on a cluster of seven hills joined together into a single village. The hills allowed the Romans to see their enemies coming.

Historians have several theories of how Italy got its name. Two have to do with cows. Ancient Romans may have called the southern part of the peninsula Italia, which means "grazing area." Or the country could have taken its name from *vitulus*, the Latin word for "cow." A third theory is that Italy was named for an early, respected leader named Italus. Take your pick.

Your journey to Rome will begin at a point midway down the western coast of the Italian Peninsula, which projects out of the southern European continent into the Mediterranean Sea. From here, where the Tiber River empties into the sea, you'll need to hop on a boat and travel about fifteen miles inland. Rome's inland position is another reason that the city's location is tops: pirates, who were a constant threat during ancient times, weren't as likely to travel up the river.

The Romans are not alone on the Italian Peninsula. Other people, such as the Etruscans and Greeks, settled there over the years, too. For a while, Rome was under the rule and influence of the Etruscan kings. But long before the Pax Romana began, the Romans bounced the kings out, formed their own republic, and took over the peninsula.

With the strength of their military, which is the most powerful in the ancient world, the Romans have built a magnificent empire. Along the way, they've enriched their culture by adopting the skills and ideas of people whom they have conquered, especially the Greeks.

THE ETERNAL CITY

When you arrive in Rome, sometime during the Pax Romana (27 B.C.–A.D. 180), the city is home to nearly one million people. Rome's growth and earlier civil unrest have created crowded conditions and other urban problems. Still, Rome's citizens regard it as the Eternal City. They believe that it will and should last forever. Once you get your bearings, you will see why Romans feel this way.

The heart of the city is the forum. This spot is where both the government and the people conduct much of their business. This is where the Senate meets, trials are held, and records kept. Romans gather here to listen to famous speakers, celebrate military victories and religious holidays, and just to hang out.

Hot Hint

Rome actually has more than one central forum. Several extra forums are built near the original Roman Forum to make room for the huge crowds that gather there. These additional forums, built by various emperors, are often called the Imperial Forums.

The Roman Forum consists of an open square surrounded by government buildings, temples, and monuments.

Overlooking the forum, from the south, is the Palatine, one of Rome's seven hills. This is the high-rent district. You'll find the most beautiful villas in the city here, including palaces built by the emperors. Other temples, monuments, and public structures are scattered across and below the other hills. The Servian Wall encloses this part of the city.

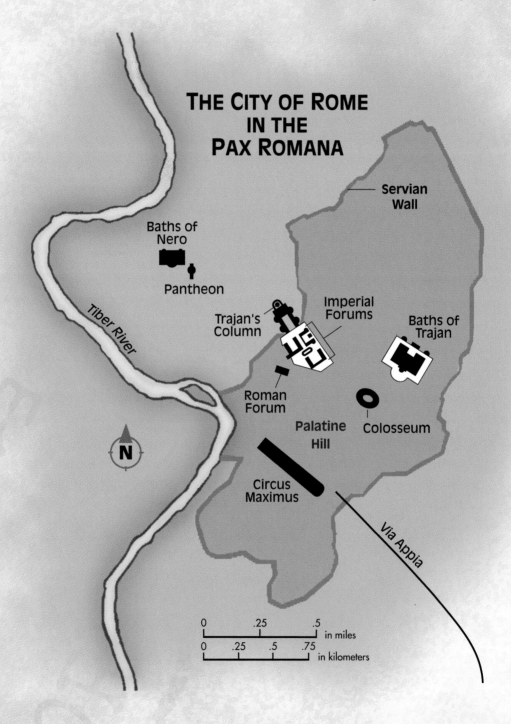

THE CITY OF ROME
IN THE
PAX ROMANA

Servian Wall

Baths of Nero

Pantheon

Tiber River

Trajan's Column

Imperial Forums

Baths of Trajan

N

Roman Forum

Palatine Hill

Colosseum

Circus Maximus

Via Appia

| 0 | .25 | .5 | in miles |

| 0 | .25 | .5 | .75 | in kilometers |

In this Roman relief (a carving on a stone surface), laborers pound stones into place to pave a road.

As soon as he becomes emperor (27 B.C.), Augustus does some badly needed fixing up in and around the city. Workers rebuild roads, clean up the Tiber River, and improve the sewage system. Existing aqueducts are repaired and new ones are built to supply the city's growing population with enough clean water. The emperor orders the construction of new public buildings, monuments, and temples and the renovation of old ones. He says, with pride, that he transformed the city from brick to marble. Augustus is smart enough to keep the home team happy. Many of the later emperors follow his example. They provide beautiful and expensive baths, graceful fountains, sports arenas, and other facilities for public use. This makes the common folks feel appreciated and less likely to rebel against their leaders and other wealthy Romans.

ON ROMAN TIME

You've probably seen the abbreviations B.C. (before the birth of Christ) and A.D. (after the birth of Christ, from *anno Domini*, Latin for "in the year of the Lord"). Or, you might be familiar with other abbreviations, such as B.C.E. (before the common era) and C.E. (of the common era). But whatever method you use to refer to the year, the ancient Romans won't understand you. Until the very end of the empire, they describe the years, rather than number them. Often, they designate years by the reign of a particular emperor or an important event.

You should feel comfortable with the months and days of the Roman calendar, though. Called the Julian calendar, it is very close to calendars that you've seen before: 365 days, grouped into twelve months, with the number of days per month varying slightly. Even the Latin names for the months, such as Aprilis and Junius, will be familiar.

One thing might confuse you. Romans refer to any given day by its relationship to the closest of three points in the month: the Kalends, the Nones, and the Ides. The Kalends is always the first day of the month. The Nones is around the end of the first week of the month, and the Ides is around the middle of the month. The Nones and the Ides shift a bit, according to the number of days in the month.

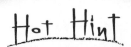

Handy WORDS & PHRASES

When major adjustments were made to the official Roman calendar in 46 B.C., the year was called The Year of Confusion.

Hot Hint

The Kalends, Nones, and Ides in the Roman calendar originally marked phases of the moon. A Roman will refer to March 23 as the tenth day before the Kalends of April. (Both March 23 and April 1 are included in the count.) This date is abbreviated and written as X Kal. Apr.

Shadow Clocks & Clocks That Drip

If you like to count only sunny hours, you'll need no better timepiece than the Roman sundial, or shadow clock. At its most basic, the sundial is usually a flat, round stone divided into twelve segments, each numbered for an hour of the day. An upright piece called a gnomon sits in the middle of the stone.

As the Earth rotates around the Sun during the day, the gnomon's shadow moves across the segments. Look for the number of the segment where the shadow ends, and you've got the time of day—sort of. Factors such as the season and where you are in the empire need to be considered for accurate timekeeping. But don't worry. In ancient Rome, nobody cares exactly what time it is.

This bowl-shaped sundial is only one of various designs the Romans used for telling time by the Sun's shadow. The indentation at the top marks where the gnomon was once located.

If you want a timepiece that works without the Sun, try a Roman water clock. This clock is a lot like an hourglass, except that it uses water instead of sand. A simple water clock is just a jar with a hole in the bottom. Horizontal lines, corresponding to the hours of the day, are painted on the side. Before you get the clock, a clockmaker has filled the jar with water and measured how much the water level drops in one hour as the water drips or trickles out of the hole. This measurement determines where the lines are painted on the jar. Find where the water level is, and you've got the time of day—or night.

A Little Latin Goes a Long Way

As the Romans spread out across Europe and Britain, so does the Latin language. That's why you already know the Latin alphabet. By the time you arrive, the Romans use an alphabet that's pretty close to the modern English one. Even though English is not a Romance language, many of its words are based on Latin. This means that you will understand bits of the Latin you hear spoken or see written during your visit. Sometimes, you'll hear Romans say whole words or phrases in Latin that sound familiar, such as *legal*, *maximum*, or *e pluribus unum* ("one out of many"—look for this phrase on modern money).

Back to the Future

Even though Latin has not been in common use since the 1500s, it's still with us. The names of all of our modern military ranks, from private to general, come from Latin. Many scientific terms, such as *gravity*, *laboratory*, and *atom* do, too. P.S., at the end of a letter, is short for the Latin term *postscriptus*. Same with A.M. and P.M., short for *ante meridiem* (before noon) and *post meridiem* (after noon). And don't forget "R.I.P.": *requiescat in pace*, or "rest in peace."

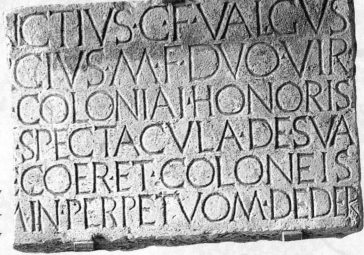

The letters cut into the stone on this fragment of a Roman sign remain clear to read in modern times.

You may not know how to use Roman numbers, but you've probably seen them before—on clocks, in some books, or on old buildings, for instance. The Romans use seven symbols from their alphabet to stand for numbers. These symbols, called Roman numerals, can be written alone to represent seven different numbers: I (1), V (5), X (10), L (50), C (100), D (500), and M (1,000). Or they can be grouped to represent many different numbers. Adding and subtracting Roman numerals isn't hard, once you get used to it. But even the Romans don't try multiplying and dividing with them. Instead, they use an abacus, a board with rows of beads that can be moved and grouped to calculate numbers.

THE NAME GAME

Romans of important families usually have at least three names: their first name, their family name, and a name that specifies their branch of the family. Only about sixteen different first names are used for boys. This means that boys have a good chance of being stuck with Publius! Fortunately, these names are so common that they're generally abbreviated when written—as in "P." for Publius. Males might also have a nickname, such as Dentitus (Toothy). Some are even worse, like Brutus (Idiot) or Verrucosus (Little Wart). And these nicknames are often carried on for generations. Once Little Wart gets started in a family, many Little Warts are likely to follow.

Women usually have only a single name. A girl is generally given the feminine form of her father's name. Octavius, for example, would name his daughter Octavia. If he has a second daughter, she'll be Octavia, too, but with the addition of a descriptive phrase, such as "the Younger." The emperor is commonly known by just one name, too. His power is so absolute that one name says it all.

19

WHICH CITIES TO VISIT

Sailors lower the sails on a Roman ship in this relief. Many ships stop at Ostia, the empire's most important commercial port.

OSTIA

As you enter the Tiber River on your way from the Mediterranean Sea to Rome, you will pass by the city of Ostia. If you're not in a big hurry, take a few hours to look around. This is the empire's main commercial port. Much of the trade conducted between Rome and areas under its control, called provinces, is done here. You will see huge warehouses on either side of the river.

Rome demands taxes from its provinces. In the case of North Africa and Egypt, these taxes are partly paid in grain. Since transport by water is the cheapest way to go, vast amounts of grain come into Ostia, where it is stored. Later it will be transferred to barges and brought up the river to Rome.

By the time of Augustus, Romans are using more wine and olive oil than they can produce themselves. Great quantities must be imported from other places in Europe. It is shipped in large clay jars that can be stacked on top of each other and stored in Ostia's warehouses. At one time, a single clay jar of wine could be traded for a slave. You will see other imports, too, including wild animals from Africa and marble from Greece.

Like Rome, Ostia has a central forum. You'll find the offices of the shipping companies here. Look for the mosaics on the ground in front of the buildings. Mosaics are patterns, sometimes intricate, made from small pieces of tile, glass, or stone set in mortar, a type of cement. In Ostia's forum, they spell out the shipper's name and provide a picture of the type of merchandise handled. These signs allow merchants to find the best person to ship their goods. When a deal is struck, the merchant will go to the nearby Temple of Ceres to offer a sacrifice. Ceres is the Roman goddess of agriculture and the bringer of good things. Since she also brings bad things—like foul weather—merchants want to keep her happy.

POMPEII

If you have lots of time to spare before heading up the Tiber River for Rome, hire a cart and donkey and take a detour to the city of Pompeii. It's a little more than one hundred miles to the south, near the Bay of Naples. You'll find plenty of public lodging places along the way. Wealthy Romans often have homes in Pompeii, where they go to escape the problems of life in the bigger city.

Pompeii sits at the base of Mount Vesuvius and is protected by high encircling walls. Enter through one of the eight gates. Try to get here on a market day, when people crowd into the forum area to sell and buy goods and services. You'll notice that many of the buildings are whitewashed. This provides a nice background for the graffiti, which is officially allowed.

Handy WORDS & PHRASES

The word "graffiti" is from the Latin *graphium*, meaning "scrawlings or writings for public viewing."

I wonder, O wall, that you have not fallen in ruins from supporting the stupidities of so many scribblers.

—*A Pompeiian graffiti artist*

Graffiti is an inexpensive way for people to advertise goods for sale, promote politicians, post apartment and rental notices, or just make a statement. Some of the graffiti artists are professional scribes and are hired to write advertisements. Others are just amateurs, who are simply expressing themselves.

Avoid visiting Pompeii in A.D. 62, when the city is hit with an earthquake. Some buildings collapse, the water supply is disrupted, and columns and statues fall. The forum is also damaged, so market day has to be held in one corner for a while, while the rest of the forum is repaired. Some wealthy residents take the quake as a warning and move to the coast, building lavish villas overlooking the sea.

The ground trembles again in August of A.D. 79. This time the shaking is an omen of an even greater disaster. Many citizens of

IMPORTANT Safety Tip

If you are in Pompeii in August A.D. 79 and feel the ground shake, get out fast! These tremors are the only warning people in Pompeii get before nearby Mount Vesuvius erupts.

As the ash and lava from the eruption of Mount Vesuvius cooled, they formed shells around the victims' bodies. Although the bodies eventually decomposed, the shells remained, allowing modern archaeologists to make concrete casts such as the one above. Mount Vesuvius looms in the background.

Pompeii are caught by surprise when Mount Vesuvius blows its top. They die while trying to escape when a tremendous blast of volcanic matter erupts from the mountain and pours down on the town. Poisonous gases fill the air.

Hot ash covers the town and the bodies of the victims. When the ash cools and hardens, it forms a shell over the people and their artifacts, preserving them for future generations to see. There isn't much personal property left of value, though. The survivors quickly return to the city and dig out what they'd left behind. Fortune hunters burrow tunnels through the ruins and take bronzes, slabs of marble, and other remains that can be sold or traded.

MONEY MATTERS

Most Roman coins carry the likeness of an emperor. The faustina *(above) is an exception. Faustina was the beloved wife of Emperor Antoninus Pius (who reigned from A.D. 138 to 161). In his grief at her death in A.D. 141, he had millions of coins made with her image.*

A DUPONDIUS FOR YOUR THOUGHTS

The coins used for big business transactions are the aureus and the denarius. During the reign of Augustus until around A.D. 150, these coins have a high gold (aureus) or silver (denarius) content. As the empire declines and its expenses go up, Roman coins are minted with less precious metals. Copper, bronze, and brass coins are used for everyday purposes.

Roman coins are not dated. Instead, they are usually stamped with an image of the current emperor or one of his family members. Some coins are minted to commemorate important events, such as military conquests and even famous assassinations.

Roman coins are used throughout the empire and in places as far away as China. You probably won't have any Roman coins when you arrive, so you'll have to go to a money changer. They keep hours on the noisy sidewalks around the forum. You won't have any trouble finding them, but you may have trouble exchanging your own coins, since they don't contain much gold or silver. If necessary, you might get a loan. Pretend that you don't really need the money. Otherwise, the moneylender will be tempted to charge interest above the legal limit of 12 percent.

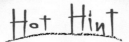

Hot Hint

You may run into some con artists in Rome. To keep your money safe, you might want to get familiar with the values of Roman coins before you go.

Coin Name	Metal	Number Equaling 1 Aureus
Aureus	Gold	1
Denarius	Silver	25
Sestertius	Brass	100
Dupondius	Brass	200
As	Bronze	400
Semis	Brass	800
Quadrans	Bronze	1,600

A WORKING WAGE

Roman workers earn a wide range of salaries. The average craftsman in the empire's first century (from about 27 B.C. to A.D. 73) makes around 60,000 sestertii a year. Manual laborers, on the other hand, may earn only between 900 and 1,200 sestertii. Soldiers didn't even earn that much until the famed military general and dictator Julius Caesar gave them a big pay raise back during his reign (49 to 44 B.C.). Army officers earn from 20,000 to 80,000 sestertii a year. A few star athletes make much more. These crowd-pleasers include charioteers, who race in horse-drawn two-wheeled carts called chariots, and gladiators, who fight others to the death.

Julius Caesar ruled Rome from 49 to 44 B.C. Standing on the back of a chariot, he addresses his soldiers. Even after he increased their pay, soldiers throughout the Roman Empire during the Pax Romana earned little compared to skilled workers.

A charioteer risked being thrown from the chariot during tight turns.

Now Hear This

Toward the end of the Pax Romana, the great charioteer Gaius Appuleius Diocles pulls in an average of around 1.5 million sestertii a year over the course of his career. His total career earnings are estimated at 35 million sestertii.

A small bag of wheat costs only a couple of sestertii, but during the first century A.D., nearly 200,000 Roman citizens receive free grain from the government to help them get by. Others may need the help but don't get it. And, of course, slaves earn only what their owner wants to give them—which could be nothing at all.

HOW TO GET AROUND

A paved road in Pompeii remains intact in modern times.

BY LAND

You won't have any trouble traveling from place to place in the empire. Romans love to build, and roads are their specialty. Over time they will build approximately 50,000 miles of major roads connecting the cities on the Italian Peninsula, as well as the farthest reaches of the empire. Extending out from the major roads are thousands of miles of smaller connecting roads, giving the people good access to towns and cities other than their own.

Roman engineers use materials and designs suited to the surface they're building on. If you look carefully at a Roman road, you may notice that its center is slightly higher than its edges. This allows rainwater to run off the road's surface into drainage ditches dug along its side, so the road remains passable in bad weather and requires less maintenance. Roman bridges are tough too—they're made of concrete and stone and supported by arches. The Romans use this vast transportation network of roads and bridges to move their armies about easily and to send official messages and other mail. The roads also ensure good transport for commercial goods and give citizens a way to travel and sightsee.

Roman-engineered arches, known for their beauty and strength, support the Milvio Bridge that crosses the Tiber River.

Tech Talk

The Romans perfect a concrete that does not need to dry out to set and can even be used underwater. (Very useful when building bridges!) Workers make the concrete by mixing a volcanic ash called pozzolana with limestone, sand, and water.

Whenever possible, Romans are on the move. As you travel through the empire, you'll see soldiers, farmers, merchants, private messengers, and others traveling to do their business. You may also meet other tourists, heading for the mountains or ocean or just sightseeing. People travel according to their means and needs. Farmers and merchants often use a wagon pulled by mules. Men who can afford horses ride them. Some wealthy people recline on a litter, a sort of travel bed, and let their slaves carry them on their shoulders. Or they might ride in an ornate silk-lined carriage pulled by mules. The soldiers walk.

Need to spend the night on the road? Try one of the many public hostelries along the way. These informal hotels provide both food and lodging. Or, plan ahead like the rich folks do and bring your own tent and supplies. Of course, you'll need a few servants to carry your goods and to keep strangers from stealing them.

Wealthy Romans often order slaves to carry them on litters from one place to the next.

Travel by road is direct and easy, but lots of robbers are lying in wait. Like most sensible Romans, you might want to break up your trip by traveling on the rivers wherever you can. It's harder for thieves to hide on the water.

BY WATER

The Romans have the greatest fleet of merchant ships in the ancient world. They transport goods from all the cities on the Mediterranean Sea. They also sail the major rivers of the empire, such as the Nile, the Danube, the Rhine—and of course, Rome's own river, the Tiber. Roman merchants travel the Indian Ocean, ranging as far east as Vietnam and China.

If you stopped in Ostia on your way to Rome, you may have noticed the *corbitas*, the most commonly seen merchant ships. They're big and slow, but they do the job. You'll see smaller merchant sailing ships, too.

The open seas can be dangerous. Never travel by sea between November and March. (You probably couldn't find anyone foolish enough to take you, anyway.) The water is far too rough. Since you're visiting during the Pax Romana, you'll be pretty safe from pirates who cruise the Mediterranean. The empire's navy keeps a careful watch during these years and has greatly reduced piracy, especially along the Italian coast. But merchants and their ships are still at risk. And pirates don't just take the cargo—they make huge profits by grabbing people and selling them into slavery. They may also kill the entire crew or hold wealthier sea travelers for ransom.

Hot Hint

Except along very well traveled routes, such as Brundisium to Greece, most of the ships you see carry cargo, not people. You can usually arrange passage on a merchant vessel, though. You'll be out on the deck, so if you want shelter, bring something you can use as a tent. And, don't forget to pack some food. Water is generally available from the crew.

LOCAL CUSTOMS
& MANNERS

WHAT YOU CAN EXPECT FROM THE LOCALS

Romans rule, so they will expect you to know something about their history and government. By the time you arrive, they've defeated every power around and have for a long time regarded the Mediterranean Sea as *mare nostrum,* or "our sea." This sense of ownership extends to the people and land around the sea.

Still, Roman society is far from perfect. The social classes are sharply divided according to wealth and family connections. Women do not have the same rights as men. Slavery is accepted, even encouraged. With the exception of joining the military, the poor have few chances to improve their prospects. Rather than providing an effective aid program for the poor, the government gives them free entertainment and an occasional sack of grain.

During its long period as a republic (509–27 B.C.), Rome was run by citizens, not one all-powerful emperor. But even then, the common folks, or plebeians, had to fight for a role in their government. The heart of the republic was the Roman Senate, which made the laws and handled the money. At first, the senators were all patricians—people who came from the richest and most powerful families. When plebeians finally gained their share of political power, they made changes to benefit the poor. These reforms, along with the expansion of the empire, made it possible for some non-patricians to prosper in areas such as foreign trade and land ownership. These newly rich businessmen gained quite a bit of political influence. But they rarely used that influence to help the poor. So, despite the

The Roman Senate in session

33

The outstanding race in the whole world is undoubtedly the Roman.

—*Pliny the Elder* (A.D. 23–79),
Roman author and statesman

success of these few, the gap between Rome's rich and poor continued to widen. Civil unrest increased. Military generals took control, and power passed from the republic to a series of dictators. These dictators were later called emperors.

Rome's most famous dictator was Julius Caesar (ca. 100–44 B.C.). You'll still hear people talk about him when you visit. Caesar was a skilled military leader and an extremely able and ambitious politician. But a group of senators didn't like it when he had himself appointed Dictator for Life. In hopes of restoring the republic—and their own control of it—they assassinated him on March 15 (known as the Ides of March), 44 B.C. He received at least twenty stab wounds from the assassins, some of whom he had believed to be his friends. This event caused civil war and a bloody struggle for power.

Julius Caesar's nephew and adopted heir, Octavian, won the struggle, and the empire officially begins. However, unlike Uncle Julius, Octavian carefully avoids titles such as dictator or emperor. He agrees to be called Augustus, which means "honored one," but gives himself the modest title of First Citizen. Victory celebrations, he decides, are getting out of hand—inspiring too much loyalty to individuals. Following their victories, new military heroes are encouraged to return to the city on horseback, or better still, to walk back. No more grand entrances in speeding chariots to excite the crowds. Augustus continues to call his government a republic and keeps some of the old offices and formalities. He listens to the Senate with respect. But his power is absolute. If you are in Rome between 27 B.C. and A.D. 14, watch for him during parades, celebrations, and other official gatherings. He'll be the one wearing a purple toga.

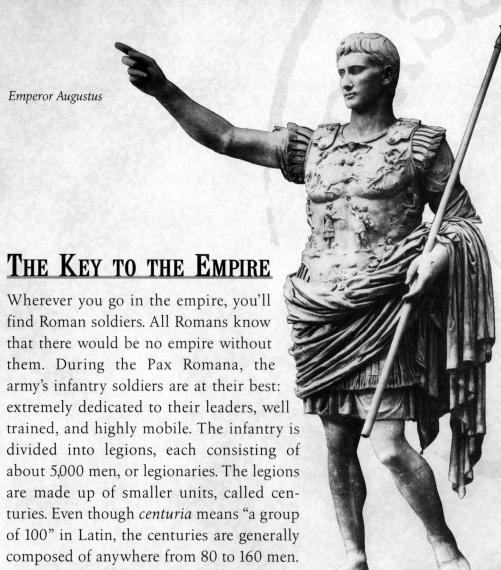

Emperor Augustus

THE KEY TO THE EMPIRE

Wherever you go in the empire, you'll find Roman soldiers. All Romans know that there would be no empire without them. During the Pax Romana, the army's infantry soldiers are at their best: extremely dedicated to their leaders, well trained, and highly mobile. The infantry is divided into legions, each consisting of about 5,000 men, or legionaries. The legions are made up of smaller units, called centuries. Even though *centuria* means "a group of 100" in Latin, the centuries are generally composed of anywhere from 80 to 160 men.

Army life is tough. Legionaries must sign on for a period of twenty years and then serve additional time as a reserve who may be called upon to serve in emergencies, often in places far away from home. But the Roman

Tech Talk

To build up strength, infantry soldiers practice fighting with swords and shields twice as heavy as those they'll use in combat. They carry about ninety pounds of gear and weapons when they march.

army's training and discipline produce soldiers who are down-right deadly in hand-to-hand combat. In a group, they are almost unstoppable.

Roman soldiers do much more than wage battles. They also build roads, walls, and other public structures throughout the empire, as well as guard all its borders.

Don't Miss

. . . Trajan's Column. One of Rome's most spectacular military memorials, Trajan's Column *(right)* is still standing. Located near the forum, the 100-foot tower has detailed carvings on its surface that depict battle scenes from the emperor Trajan's victories in the early 100s A.D. These scenes are valuable tools for historians studying the battles, armor, fortifications, and equipment of Roman soldiers.

The legionaries use an attack technique called the tortoise. By closing ranks and locking their shields together, they create a protective shell over their bodies. This allows them to get close to the walls of an enemy city or fort. Another wave of soldiers then closes in with ladders, ramps, and portable towers.

The Roman legions are helped by auxiliary (extra) soldiers recruited from the conquered lands. The auxiliaries have skills perfected by their own people and often serve as specialized troops, such as archers and cavalrymen (soldiers on horseback). By A.D. 100, they are a vital part of the army.

Roman citizens celebrate the military's victories with great enthusiasm. Homecoming warriors march in grand processions through the rejoicing city. Try not to get squashed when the crowds pour onto the streets, waving their arms and shouting. At the head of the parade is the conquering general. Romans often build memorials, such as arches, to further honor their military heroes.

You'll be glad you're not one of the Romans' unfortunate captives—they are sometimes paraded through the city and publicly executed. Others are sold into slavery. An even worse fate awaits Roman soldiers who have not fought well. Military officials randomly select one of every ten men from underperforming units. The chosen soldiers are beaten to death by their fellow legionaries.

Handy Words & Phrases

The word *decimate*, which means "to cause great destruction," comes from the Roman army's practice of killing one-tenth of those soldiers who fight without enough enthusiasm. In Latin, *decimus* means "tenth."

No one is more aware of the importance of the military than Augustus who, like Julius Caesar before him, strives to improve army conditions. He trims the number of legions from sixty to a more manageable twenty-eight and increases bonuses and other benefits.

Most conquering forces around this time hit their target hard, thoroughly destroy it, and go home, taking everything of value with them. Romans grab whatever is valuable, too. But, unlike most other armies, they leave plenty of their own soldiers and officials behind to establish new towns or improve old ones. They include the conquered lands, which become known as the provinces, in the empire. Many retired legionaries never go back to Rome. Instead, they stay in the provinces on land given to them by the emperor. They raise families, spread the Latin language, and watch out for Roman interests. This system is another reason that the empire lasts as long as it does.

The Pont-du-Gard in southern France is one of many aqueducts that Roman soldiers build throughout the empire. These durable structures carry water from rural hills to towns and cities.

GIVE A LITTLE, TAKE A LOT

If you travel beyond the Italian Peninsula to other parts of the empire, you'll see that, for some folks, being defeated by the Romans actually has its up side. True, the conquered people lose most of their money and a lot of their land. They have to pay big taxes to Rome. And there's always the chance that they'll end up somebody's slave. Still, those who survive to become Roman subjects have new opportunities for trade with the rest of the empire. They get to use the well-built Roman roads to transport their goods. They also get Roman-built aqueducts, theaters, and other public structures.

In fact, in your travels through the empire, you may have trouble telling the invaders from the "invadees." Many of the conquered have become so Romanized that they speak Latin and dress just like Romans. Some also serve as auxiliaries to the Roman army and even become official Roman citizens.

Rome doesn't have to gain the entire empire by force. Some local rulers and tribal leaders willingly turn over their power and people to the Romans. This way, they get the benefits of being part of the empire without having to confront the Roman military.

SLAVERY

Slavery is a fact of life in Rome. Citizens do not believe it is wrong to buy and sell human beings. By the time you visit, slaves make up a huge part of Rome's workforce. Most have been brought back to Rome as prisoners of war from conquered lands. Romans also buy slaves from pirates, who sell their captives at the slave

This nineteenth-century engraving depicts Roman slaves being sold to the highest bidder.

Many Roman slaves had humble jobs, such as pouring wine at meals in Roman homes.

markets. Some slaves come from families forced by debt or poverty to place their children up for sale.

Because slaves come from such diverse backgrounds, they have many different skills. They are doctors, teachers, tradesmen, and actors. Slaves also work at difficult, dangerous tasks, such as mining or laboring as oarsmen on merchant ships. Some merchants own not only the ship and cargo—they own the entire crew. All on board, including the captain, are slaves. Other slaves are forced daily to fight for their lives as gladiators. But many Romans treat their slaves kindly, even paying them a salary. Eventually, some owners either give their slaves freedom or allow the slaves to buy it. Some of these freed slaves become Roman citizens.

Roman law deals harshly with slaves who run away, commit crimes against their owners, or take part in uprisings. Those who try to escape may be tortured or killed if caught.

Some Romans oppose such harsh penalties for slaves. In A.D. 61, a mob of angry Romans rushed to the Senate to protest a sentence passed when a slave killed his owner. Not only was the murderer sentenced to death—all of the four hundred other slaves in the household were, too. Although some senators tried to stop it, the sentence was carried out anyway.

Antoninus Pius

Now Hear This

If you arrive in Rome in the later years of the Pax Romana, you'll see more Romans concerned about the rights of slaves. The emperors Domitian (who reigned from A.D. 81 to 96) and Antoninus Pius (who reigned from A.D. 138 to 161) pass laws protecting certain rights of slaves.

Day-to-Day Life

Every Roman husband and father is emperor in his own household. Wives are expected to obey their husbands and behave in a polite and reserved way in public. Women cannot vote, hold public office, or take part in public discussions. But some become very rich, despite occasional laws that restrict what they can own. Privately, many men are greatly influenced by their wives. Even Augustus seeks, and often takes, his wife Livia's advice on political issues. Her behind-the-scenes power continues when her son becomes emperor after Augustus dies.

You may think of heading home early when you learn about kids' rights in the Roman Empire. There aren't any. Roman law gives a father total control over his children. His sons cannot own property until he dies. He must give his approval for his children to marry, and he has the power to end any of their marriages. If someone comes along from a family with better connections, a father can force a son or daughter to divorce spouse #1 and marry the new candidate. After 37 B.C., however, the law forbids marriages of children under a certain age: girls must be at least twelve, boys must be fourteen. Even the most eager father must wait until his children reach the legal age. Then he's free to place them in arranged marriages that improve the family's finances or power.

It gets even worse. Fathers even have the legal right to sell their children as slaves, have them sent away, or put to death. Although few fathers use these rights, most kids know that it is best to stay on good terms with papa.

Now Hear This

At one time, children could be used as collateral for a debt. That meant that the lender kept the child until the loan was paid.

One thing you might envy about Roman kids is that they don't have to go to school. In fact, there aren't any public schools. Children get an education only if their families can afford to pay an independent teacher.

A tutor (right) *supervises a Roman child's studies.*

Then they might attend classes in a corner of a noisy shop in the forum, or even on the sidewalk!

Wealthy boys and girls are often taught at home. Their teacher is sometimes one of the family's Greek slaves, who is likely to be better educated than any other member of the household. Children study reading, writing, and arithmetic from around the age of seven to twelve. Competitions and games, such as essay-writing contests, are encouraged. Older boys may be educated further in the art of logical argument and public speaking. Since women are not usually allowed any public life, formal education for girls generally stops earlier.

Roman girls at play crouch intently over their game (above). A Roman girl's rag doll (left) might be filled with parchment as well as rags.

For fun, girls play with dolls made from cloth, bone, or clay. Both boys and girls play marbles, hide-and-seek, tag, jacks, and board games. You may be asked to play Robbers, a game similar to chess. If you capture enough of the other player's important pieces, you win.

You might get a chance to play another popular game if you visit any of Rome's public baths. In the ball game called Trigon, three players stand in the water in a triangle,

Romans took their games of Robbers seriously. Witnesses claim that while waiting to be executed, one Roman prisoner became so involved playing Robbers that he hardly seemed to notice when the executioners dragged him away. He shouted that he was winning and that the other player had better not lie about it. He made the jailer his witness.

each one holding a ball. The idea is to try to catch the other players off guard by throwing your ball when they don't expect it. The tricky part is that they're throwing balls at you at the same time.

When visiting a Roman family, you'll probably meet their pets. Birds are very popular, including crows, magpies, and sparrows. Lots of people have fish and dogs. Cats are kept more as rodent police than as house pets.

A pet dog looks hopefully to the lady of the house for attention or a treat.

LOCAL MANNERS

While in Rome, watch your manners. Women are supposed to speak quietly and behave modestly at all times. Same goes for kids. Before joining wealthy folks for a meal, get a quick lesson on table manners from the family tutor. It's the tutor's job to teach the children proper etiquette. Since you won't find any forks on a Roman table (just spoons and knives), it's okay to eat with your fingers. But hold the food daintily between your forefinger and thumb. Don't grab, and don't reach in front of others, especially your host.

For everyday meals, some Romans used pottery dishes made of coiled clay.

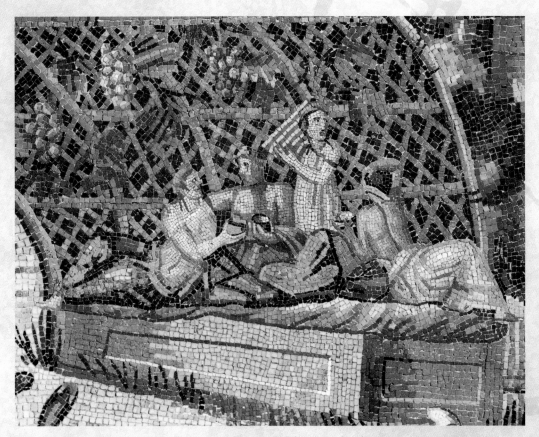

A musician (standing) *offers entertainment at a banquet for three. Roman etiquette requires removing your sandals before reclining to dine.*

Of course, unless you're somebody pretty important, you won't get that close to your host, anyway. People are arranged around the table according to social order. High-ranking men recline on couches near the host—and near the best food. Women are placed a little farther away. Children may be assigned to their own table, possibly across the room from the adults. It is considered extremely rude for adults to use bad language or display bad habits—such as excessive eating or drinking—if children are present.

LOCAL BELIEFS

Romans believe that their fates are controlled by gods and goddesses, who must be treated with respect. By the time you arrive, the Romans have adopted and renamed Greek gods and goddesses. Many Romans also worship the emperor, together with Roma, the

Part of a temple to Vesta, the Roman goddess of the home, still stands in the Roman Forum in Rome, Italy.

goddess of the city of Rome. In the A.D. 100s, some Romans become interested in religions coming from the Middle East, including Judaism and Christianity.

Romans celebrate lots of public holidays dedicated to one god or another. Work and commerce stop. Believers go to the temples to make offerings and take part in public rituals. Festivals usually have some religious meaning, but they are also a time to have fun. Try to be in Rome during the weeklong Saturnalia, which begins on December 17. The wealthy treat everyone to feasts, and the emperor provides entertainment. There is much gift giving and merrymaking, with masters sometimes even trading places with their servants.

As part of their beliefs, Romans have lots of superstitions. Augustus, for example, refuses to travel on the Nones of any month. For him, the word *Nones* is simply too close to the Latin *non is*, which in English means "you do not go."

Romans also take lots of charms and curses seriously. Parents give each of their children a *bulla*, or lucky charm, to wear until their teens. To inflict bad luck, people write curses—along with the names of the unlucky recipients—on thin sheets of lead called curse tablets. To ensure the fullest impact, the sender hires a professional curse writer to handle the transaction. He or she will bury the tablet, place it in an appropriate temple, or, sometimes, drop it down a well. From there the tablet does its dark work.

Hot Hint

Here are some common Roman superstitions.

To Ensure Good Luck:
- When people sneeze, always wish them *bona salus* (good health).
- Trim your nails on market day. Don't speak while doing this.
- Always spit on your right shoe before you put it on.

To Avoid Bad Luck:
- When a guest gets up to leave, do not get out your broom and sweep the floor.
- Do not say the word *fire* during a banquet. (If you do, this slip can be fixed by spilling water on the floor.)

DEATH & BEYOND

Some Roman citizens may live to be one hundred years old or even older, especially those who are from wealthy families. But death comes early for most people. Infant and child mortality rates are high. On average, married women will probably live only thirty-four years, and married men only forty-six. Ancient Rome keeps no official written records for life expectancy. Estimates come mostly from costly grave inscriptions, so they only reflect the life spans of wealthier members of the population. The poor probably had a much shorter life expectancy.

When someone dies, the family or servants of the deceased wash the body and rub it with oils or perfume and dress it. They may slip a coin into the mouth to cover any possible travel expenses.

Hot Hint

Some Romans believe that the dead must cross a mythical river to get to their final resting place. The coin placed in a dead Roman's mouth will pay for his or her ferry ride across that river.

Romans believe that, although the body dies, the spirit lives on. They don't agree on just where it takes up residence, however. Some believe that the spirit goes up to the heavens or down into the earth. Others believe that it stays near the site where the body is buried and needs to be cared for. These folks bring the spirit food and drink, which they sometimes deliver through tubes that run down from the grave's surface to the buried body.

In this relief of a Roman funeral procession, the deceased woman lies on a fancy couch carried by mourners and slaves. She gazes at the heavens, the direction some Romans believe the spirit goes after death.

To mark the graves of their loved ones, wealthy people build fancy monuments. A rich Roman's grave marker usually consists of a likeness of the deceased carved into the tombstone. The person's name, dates of birth and death, and possibly a message are also written in the stone. Poorer families mark graves with clay pitchers or small urns, where they place simple offerings such as bread and wine.

Rich or poor, everybody's grave lies outside of Rome. Burials are not allowed within the city limits, so the family of a deceased person has to take the body away to be buried. The wealthy go in style. During your visit, you might see a funeral parade passing through Rome. The body is laid upon a couch in a reclining position and paraded along the streets, followed by a stream of mourners and musicians. Some of the mourners are professionals, hired by the family to wail in grief as they pass through the city. Family members may wear masks resembling the deceased or other ancestors. Usually the group stops at the forum, giving the deceased a final visit to every Roman's favorite gathering place.

WHAT TO WEAR

THE WELL-DRESSED ROMAN

If you don't want to look like a tourist, pack plenty of plain, oversized T-shirts. These will pass for the comfortable, loose garment, or tunic, worn by many Romans—kids and adults alike. A man's tunic stops at his knees. Underneath he wears a loincloth, which is wraparound underwear. To go out, he might wear the toga, the traditional garment worn only by a Roman citizen. In bad weather, he may throw a hooded cloak, sometimes made of leather, over his shoulders to keep warm and dry.

Although a toga looks really sharp when it is draped properly over the tunic, it's no fun to wear one. A toga is bigger than it looks—it can be up to 20 feet by 10 feet—and it's heavy, too. Getting it on right is a two-person job. Depending on the way it is draped, only one of the wearer's hands may be left free. The other is holding up the toga! Many men find the toga so uncomfortable that they refuse to wear it. Laws passed by various emperors requiring all male citizens to wear the toga in public are often ignored.

In Rome's early days, women also wore togas. But by the time you visit, most of them wear pleated tunics that go all the way to the floor. Women's tunics may or may not have sleeves. Over their tunics, women wear the *stola*. A stola is a long, flowing garment that is belted around the waist. If the weather is bad, a Roman woman may also wear a cloak.

Roman men wear black togas to funerals, but most of their togas, as well as their other clothes, are white. Nobody but the emperor and a few very high-ranking officials wear purple togas, although some togas may have a purple stripe.

The husband and wife shown here are wearing typical ancient Roman clothing. The man clutches his toga with one hand. The woman wears a stola, and she has a cloak draped over her shoulders and head to protect herself from the weather.

To keep their whites bright, most wealthy folks send them out to a laundry shop, called a *fullery*. Fullery workers wash the clothes in a powerful cleaning solution that includes urine. The high ammonia content of the urine, together with clay, potash, and carbonate of soda, will put the sparkle back in anybody's toga. The shop gets plenty of urine from its employees, or from passersby who know that a fullery is always a good pit stop. Although the clothes smell fine by the time they're finished, the neighborhood of the fullery is another matter. A certain aroma hovers in the air.

Poor folks may own a toga but usually wear a tunic. Since fullery services are expensive, their clothes quickly take on a tinge of gray or brown.

Romans wear sandals wherever they can. Even soldiers wear them. Military sandals lace up over the ankle and may have short, blunt nails, called hobnails, in the soles to prevent slipping. When their feet need more protection, Romans sometimes wear leather boots.

Lookin' Good

Most Roman men keep their hair short, so they don't have to bother with it. But many worry about baldness and, regardless of social class or rank, will go to great lengths to conceal it. For an expert on the subject, look up the emperor Domitian during his reign, anytime between A.D. 81 and 96. Not only did he write a book on the problem of baldness, he has a great solution: he simply decrees that hair must be added to any image made of him.

Roman women braid or twist their hair into elaborate patterns held in place by combs or a hair net. A very wealthy woman might even sprinkle her hair with gold dust. Some women go bald from bleaching or coloring agents. No problem—they just rub their heads with bear fat and put on wigs instead.

Rome's wealthy, such as Faustina the Younger, set the trends in hairstyling. These trends change so often in Rome that sculpted busts of people are sometimes made in two pieces: the head and the hair. The hair can be removed and resculpted in the latest style.

54

TAKE IT
from a Local

A wealthy Roman woman has a long morning beauty routine. First she washes off the antiwrinkle paste she applied to her face the night before. The paste may be a simple mixture of flour and water. Or it may be more exotic stuff—such as honey, ground-up flower bulbs, and the crushed antlers of a wild stag. Then, after soaking in the tub, she has her special servant, called an *unctor*, rub her body with oils to soften her skin. Then she's likely to apply facial makeup. This makeup consists of white powder, rouge, and, finally, a dab of wood ash for eye shadow.

You'll notice that Roman women also like to wear jewelry, such as bracelets, necklaces, and earrings made of many different materials, including gold and silver. They also like cameos carved from ivory or bone, which show a loved one's face from the side. Cameos are worn as necklaces or decorative pins. A married woman often wears a large, gold wedding ring, with an outline of two hands clasped together. This design represents her loyalty to her husband. A man doesn't usually wear a wedding ring, but he may wear a signet ring with a personalized symbol carved in it. When the ring is pressed into a soft substance, such as wax, the symbol is imprinted in it. This serves as the wearer's signature on official documents.

Roman hairpins, jewelry, and cosmetics fill this decorative case.

WHAT TO
SEE & DO

The Pantheon was built to honor the highest-ranking Roman gods and goddesses.

TEMPLE WITH THE HOLE ON TOP

One of your first stops in the city of Rome should be the Pantheon, a temple dedicated to the most important Roman deities (gods and goddesses). The temple was first built by Augustus in 27 B.C., but this isn't the Pantheon you want to see. If you wait another one hundred years or so, you'll find a later, spectacular version built by the emperor Hadrian. Hadrian keeps the original, rectangular portico (a big porch) and places behind it a round, windowless temple with a domed roof. Some Romans don't like the idea of joining rectangular structures with round ones and find the Pantheon's exterior unpleasant and chaotic. But everybody agrees that the building's interior is a masterpiece. Everything—columns, arches, recessed panels in the ceiling and walls, you name it—comes together in perfect harmony beneath the dome at the top, which is thought to weigh approximately five thousand tons.

In the center of the dome is a large hole open to the sky, which is the temple's only source of light. The Romans believe that being able to see the sky from within the temple links them with the heavens. They call the hole the oculus, or eye. What if it rains? The floor is sloped just a little toward a drain in the middle of the temple.

SIDE TRIP TRIVIA

Romans have the earliest known guidebook, produced in A.D. 22. It gives travel information about the major tourist attractions in Greece.

Back TO THE FUTURE

Nobody has ever figured out exactly how the Romans built the Pantheon. Its dome *(above)* is a single span of concrete 142 feet in diameter and forms half of a perfect sphere. The temple is so well constructed that you can still visit it and see the dome nearly two thousand years later.

As you travel, you may feel like the miles are going by awfully quickly. They are! One Roman mile is only 4,790 feet, compared to our modern mile of 5,280 feet.

VENTURE DOWN THE VIA APPIA

If you want to take a day trip, pick up one of the maps available to travelers and head south out of the city down the Via Appia, also known as the Appian Way. In 312 B.C., the Romans began building their finest road, the Via Appia. When it's finished, it extends from Rome to the port of Brundisium on the Adriatic coast, where travelers depart

The Appian Way, lined with tombs and other monuments to the dead, was one of the empire's most impressive roads, as well as one of its busiest.

IMPORTANT
Safety Tip

You can still walk along
segments of the Via Appia. Just
as in ancient times, watch
out for traffic.

for Greece. You will see milestones all along the way. Even the most confused traveler cannot miss them. From six to thirteen feet in height, these flat, upright stones are engraved with the distances from one point to another.

The Via Appia's level surface is a mosaic of multisided paving stones so well fit together that they need no mortar. The surface is meant to go easy on wheels—and especially soldiers' feet—but it is also very pretty. As late as the end of the Roman Empire, in A.D. 476, it still looks good.

A trip down the Via Appia can be uncomfortable, though. If you travel in the summer, it gets hot. There isn't much shade, and some of the marshier areas have lots of mosquitoes. The road can get crowded, too, as merchants, soldiers, and sightseers travel in and out of the city. Step aside when you see a group of slaves running ahead of their master's carriage or litter. They are under orders to clear the way. In hot weather, the wealthy move household goods, food, and servants down the Via Appia to their country villas in the cooler temperatures of the hills or seaside.

It's unlikely that you'll be invited to hop on a litter with a wealthy traveler—even if you felt comfortable being carried by others. But you might hitch a ride on a farm wagon. Or, like the military, you can simply walk. Do not go alone. Your chances of being robbed along the Via Appia are high.

If you get tired, stop to rest at one of the many cemeteries by the side of the road and sit in the shade behind a tombstone. By reading some of the inscriptions, you'll see how short life could be for the ancient Romans.

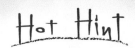

Hot Hint

During the first century A.D., Romans learn the art of glassblowing. By blowing through a long tube, a skilled craftsperson can easily change the size and shape of liquid glass without being burned by the heat source. Glassware becomes much more advanced in Rome and throughout the empire.

This dark blue glass bowl and pitcher are from Pompeii. They were probably created by a skilled glassblower for the banquet table.

GO AHEAD, HAVE A PEARL

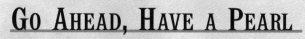

If you are invited to a Roman feast, pack a sandwich.
Many of the items on the menu will not appeal to you. You may hesitate, for example, to chow down on the ostrich brains. How about a peahen's egg stuffed with sparrow meat? Lampreys are also considered a great treat. Many wealthy Romans breed these eel-like fish in their private ponds to serve at their banquets. Another tasty favorite is dormouse, a small rodent. Dormice are usually served stuffed with pork bits and pepper.

Along with the sandwich, be sure to pack your own napkin. It is considered extremely rude to show up without one.

At certain times during Rome's heyday, banquets become so extravagant that some emperors pass laws setting limits on what could be spent. The laws are pretty much ignored. So don't be surprised if you are offered a pearl to eat. During the early days of the empire, it is fashionable to serve them to guests. You may notice that your vegetables glitter. That's right. Grains of gold.

A Roman villa has a table in the dining room, but no chairs. When you arrive for dinner, you'll be shown to a couch, where you can recline on pillows or sit upright while eating. Once you've gotten settled in, expect the servants to do everything for you except chew. They will bring you perfumed water to wash your hands, constantly offer you delicacies from the banquet table, and cut up the food for you. If you start to sweat, they'll fan you with peacock feathers.

Romans love roses. You may find their petals raining down on your head or filling the cushions you're lying on. The wine—and even the pies—may also be made from roses. And just when you've had enough, their scent may be spread throughout the room through vents in the floor.

Oh, and forget everything you know about table manners. You may be surprised to find that belching is encouraged here, and at big banquets, vomiting—to make space for the next course—is perfectly acceptable. Don't worry. There's a special area for people who are going to hurl. Staffed by trained servants, it's called the *vomitorium*.

SIDE TRIP TRIVIA

While visiting Rome, the Egyptian queen Cleopatra bet Caesar's general, Marc Antony, that she could spend 10 million sestertii on a banquet. This was a huge sum of money (a really nice villa sold for around 3.5 million sestertii). She then plopped one of her pearl earrings in vinegar, drank it down, and easily won the bet.

Now Hear This

Not all wealthy Romans eat to excess. Emperor Augustus, although willing to hold extravagant banquets in the Roman style for guests, has simple tastes. He eats small portions of bread and cheese, with cucumber slices or lettuce—sometimes a little fish. He also likes figs. When he travels, he takes bread and some fruit, such as apples and a few dates.

You'll probably find watching the Romans gorge themselves fascinating enough, but there's professional entertainment, too. Between courses, musicians, clowns, and others will perform. At some point, the party may well get loud and disorderly. This is a good time to thank your host or hostess and leave.

BENE LAVE! HAVE A GOOD BATH!

While in Rome—or almost anyplace else in the empire—take a soak in one of the public bathhouses. It doesn't cost much (kids get in free!). You will meet people of all social ranks here, as they exercise, gossip, and get clean. Some of the bigger baths have gardens and comfortable public meeting rooms and libraries. The walls are often covered with frescoes— paintings that seem to be part of the plaster itself. The frescoes that you see in the baths usually show scenes of Roman life or the countryside.

Don't Miss

. . . fresco painters at work. They paint at top speed to get their designs onto walls while the plaster is still wet. If the plaster dries, it will no longer absorb the paints that the artist is using.

This fresco in Pompeii cleverly adds the illusion of windows to the room.

Sea creatures, including an octopus, decorate the mosaic floor of this Roman bathing room.

Pool walls may be lined with complex mosaic designs and bordered by rows of columns and statues.

When you go to the baths, first work up a good sweat in the exercise area. Wrestling matches are very popular. Or you could try a little weight lifting or boxing. Then, get an attendant to rub your skin with oil and scrape you clean with the strigil, a tool with a dull edge. There is no soap.

TAKE IT from a Local

What was worse than Nero? What was better than Nero's hot baths?

—Martial, weighing the pros and cons of life during the emperor Nero's reign (A.D. 54–68)

The baths are crowded and noisy. You'll hear a few screams and a lot of groans, as attendants who specialize in plucking out unwanted hair or giving forceful massages go to work on their clients. People shout to each other, laugh, sing, and play board games.

Hop into the *tepidarium, the* first of a series of pools. As its name suggests, this pool is filled with pleasant room-temperature water. Then move on to the *caladarium*, which is hot. Soak there awhile and listen to the gossip. Be prepared for the last pool, the *frigidarium*. No translation needed. Brrr!

Before you head out for the local bathhouse, you should be aware that the Roman sense of privacy may be different from yours. Clothing in the pools is minimal. Although some baths have separate areas—or hours—for men and women, others don't. You should also be aware that the baths are a favorite hangout of thieves. Keep an eye on your valuables.

Tech Talk

The Romans use a furnace to create hot air and then vent it into a space beneath the pools to heat the water. Some of the empire's baths, such as those in the British town of Bath, use natural hot springs to heat the water.

WHERE TO FIND
SPORTS & RECREATION

It took thousands of workers to build the Colosseum in Rome. This huge sports arena seats 50,000 people.

A GAME YOU DON'T WANT TO LOSE

Calling the gladiator battles held in the Roman amphitheaters "games" is something of a stretch. But to the Romans, this is the ultimate spectator sport. On game days, Romans of all ages and social classes fill Rome's gigantic Colosseum, the largest amphitheater in the empire.

Opening in A.D. 80–81 and added to by emperors who reigned later, the Colosseum is a model sports stadium. It is made of concrete, stone, and white marble. Eighty arched entrances are numbered to allow orderly entry and exit of up to fifty thousand spectators at a time. A canvas can be raised above the wood or marble seats to shield people from the sun and rain. The floor of the structure can be flooded for mock naval battles. Below ground are cages for the animals and cells for the human participants.

A typical game day starts with a fight to the death between wild animals pushed into the arena, or with a contest between the animals and a human hunter—often unarmed. Leopards, lions, wild boars—even elephants—are brought from Roman Africa for use in these games. Expect a few public executions of prisoners during the mid-day slowdown. Some are tied to a stake and eaten by the animals. The big show—the gladiator competition—generally comes last. Before they fight, the gladiators pass before the emperor's box and say, "Those who are about to die salute you." They know that losing this contest means being killed.

Most gladiators don't actually apply for the job. They're forced into it because they are prisoners of war, slaves, or have been found guilty of a crime. Their fighting skills are sharpened at special training facilities, which are watched over carefully by the government. (They *really* don't want these guys to organize and come after the emperor!)

Remember, Romans build their empire by defeating others in battle. They take a special interest in the tactics, skills, and courage of the desperate gladiators. When a gladiator shows great spirit, but loses, the appreciative crowd may appeal to the emperor to spare his—or her—life. (A few gladiators are women.) The emperor indicates his decision by signaling with his thumb.

Back TO THE FUTURE

There is some disagreement over which way the ancient Romans held their thumbs to indicate mercy. But these days, most people consider a thumbs-up to mean good news.

This mosaic shows Roman gladiators in their gear. While heavy armor offered protection, it slowed down gladiators. The advantage and the victory could go to someone wearing little or no armor if he or she was agile.

After a great performance, a gladiator may be given a reward or even allowed to go free. Despite the danger, some who win their freedom stay in the profession and become celebrities.

Usually sponsored by the ruling emperor, these extravaganzas of violence are meant to keep the people content. The games of the Colosseum's grand opening went on for one hundred days. All shows are free to the public, although seating is by rank. Senators and other wealthy men sit in front, other men higher up and in the middle, and women in the very back, near the top. Attendants keep the grounds tidy by raking up the blood-soaked sand during intermissions and replacing it with clean sand.

AND THEY'RE OFF!

Gladiator shows too gruesome for you? Head down to the Circus Maximus, Rome's chariot racetrack. Although you can find racetracks throughout the empire, this is the greatest of them all—it's six football fields long. By the end of the first century A.D., it has been expanded to hold 250,000 spectators. You'll know a race is going on, because the roar of the crowds can be heard for miles. Keep to the outside of the viewing crowd. Disagreements over the races and the money bet on them often lead to full-scale brawls, even deaths.

Watch the official who holds the white napkin. When he drops it, the starting gates open and the chariots burst through. You'll see four teams: the Whites, the Reds, the Blues, and the Greens. Members of each team will make seven laps around the track for each race—eight if there's a tie. Four to eight chariots compete during a race.

Four horses usually pull each chariot, although there are races with teams as small as two horses, or as big as seven. All great charioteers are superb horsemen and are quite willing to assault their opponents with a speeding vehicle. At any time, a charioteer can be thrown from his cart and trampled. But if his horses are the first to cross the finish line, he wins, dead or alive. Like the gladiators, some charioteers beat the odds and live long enough to win many races and become rich and famous. Perhaps the greatest of all is Gaius Appuleius Diocles, who wins 1,462 races and retires in his early forties as a wealthy man. To see him race, get to Rome anytime between A.D. 122 and 146.

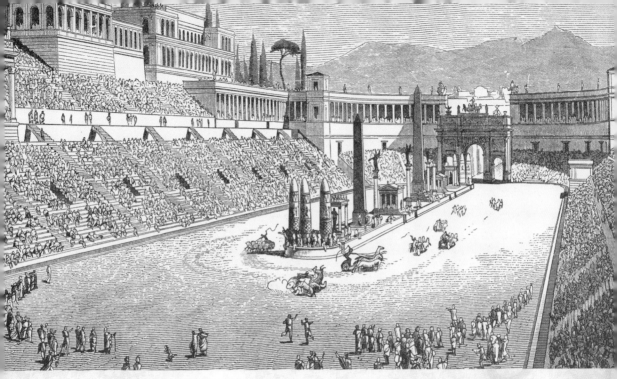
A chariot race thrills the crowd at the Circus Maximus in Rome.

TAKE IN A SHOW

If you like serious drama, you're in the wrong place. Romans write some serious plays, but they are seen mostly by private, educated audiences. It's hard to compete with the spectacle of gladiators and chariots. But comedies, especially the silent plays called mimes, are a big hit. These plays offer simple or no dialogue, but plenty of dramatic scenery and special effects, such as ghosts floating up from under the stage. They are often about Roman gods and goddesses, politics, young love, rude servants, or marital mischief. To add excitement, some theater managers may have live horses galloping through the theater or even have criminals executed during intermission.

Rome has good theaters, some with room for as many as twenty thousand people. Based on Greek designs, the seating area is built on a downward slope and curves around the stage. This design gives everybody a good view. All shows are free to the public.

Roman audiences show their approval or disapproval openly. They cheer and clap loudly and wave their handkerchiefs or the ends of their togas if they like the show. They boo and yell rude suggestions at the actors if they disapprove. Theater managers hire people to sit in the audience and applaud at the right times. The hope is that these paid fans will persuade the rest of the audience that the play is good.

WHERE TO STAY

The House of Diana in Ostia probably had several rooms to rent over its cluster of shops. You may have to settle for that kind of an inexpensive room. The best luxury apartments in the empire rent for as much as ten thousand sestertii a year—about ten times the annual salary of a manual laborer.

HEY, WHAT'S THAT SMELL?

To get a real sense of how Romans live, try to stay in a private home during your visit. Most folks live in the crowded areas of the city in multi-story tenements that are dirty and poorly maintained. The first thing you'll notice—before you even go inside—is the bad smell. Residents are supposed to take their sewage to disposal areas for removal to the city's sewage system. But some folks just tip it out the window. Indoors, things aren't much better. Because the rooms are so dark, oil lanterns are used a lot. The burning oil fills the whole building with smoke.

If you can't find anyone to stay with, check with a shopkeeper. Often shops have rooms for rent on their upper floors. But watch your step. Fights break out so frequently in quarters like these that some emperors try to close them down. Rome has a few inns, too, but their accommodations aren't a whole lot better. Be sure to get a room on the lowest floor possible—the higher the floor, the greater the danger from fire. An overturned oil lamp can easily start a blaze, and narrow stairways can make it hard to escape.

At some point in your trip, no matter where you end up staying, you'll probably have to use a public toilet. These are low, stone walls with up to twenty seats (well, actually, they're just holes) along the top.

Hot Hint

Rome's streets smell so bad at times that a wealthy woman may carry a sweet-scented ball of amber (the fossilized sap of certain kinds of trees). By rubbing it and holding it under her nose, she can block out the stench from the streets.

This twelve-seat, open-air public toilet is another example of Roman engineering excellence.

A good facility may have a gutter with water running through it in front of the wall. What's the sponge on a stick for? That's the toilet tissue. Be polite and rinse it after use. This is a good place to strike up a conversation with a Roman, since you will almost certainly have company.

Despite the smell in the city streets, most Romans spend as much time as possible outdoors, rather than inside their apartments. Some residents even cook their meals on the streets. The aroma from their stoves or pots of hot coals rises up to the apartments above, helping to mask the indoor odors.

If you want some reading material, take a look at the writing scrawled on walls in the city squares. This graffiti can be very useful. Sometimes it advertises services, goods for sale, or rooms for rent. Sometimes it's just graffiti.

The noise in the streets, especially in busy areas such as the forum, is nonstop. Vendors shout the names of their products. Street entertainers sing, play instruments, and dance. Shopkeepers announce the good prices they're offering that day. Tutors read their lessons loudly to students, who are sitting on the ground. Craftsmen hammer away at their wares. Beggars plead with the crowd, and moneychangers sit at low tables on the sidewalk and jingle their coins to attract business. Sometimes drunken soldiers and sailors are fighting.

The graffiti on this wall in Pompeii promotes a candidate for political office.

This pool, with an island in its center, is part of a villa that Emperor Hadrian built in Tivoli, Italy. The huge rural estate covered at least 250 acres and had thirty buildings.

WHICH WAY TO THE REFLECTING POOL?

If you are invited to a well-to-do citizen's villa, go. You won't feel the energy of the city's center, but you won't smell it, either. Most Roman villas have the same basic layout. When you arrive, you'll pass through the pair of front doors to the atrium, a central courtyard that has an opening in the roof to let sun come in. A large urn under the opening collects rainwater for household use. The shrine to the household gods is usually here, too. The family will visit the shrine each day, asking for protection for their household.

All the rooms of the house open onto the atrium. They have very little furniture. You may see a couch or bed for sleeping or reclining. You might also see a table or footstool, but no chairs. In contrast to this simplicity, the walls of nearly every room will be decorated with frescoes, like the Roman baths. The floors often have elaborate mosaic designs and scenes.

You'll usually find a lovely garden at the back of the house, with clipped hedges, fountains, a row of statues or columns, and possibly a reflecting pool. You may want to sit on a bench and reflect a moment on the sharp contrast between the villa and the tenements you've seen.

WHAT TO EAT

These Romans buy bread at a bakery.

THREE SQUARES A DAY

As a visitor, you may get the chance to attend a feast. But most Romans never get invited to a real banquet. They have very simple diets compared to those of the wealthy. They eat three meals a day, made up of breads, cereals, and fruits and vegetables, including pears, grapes, peas, and beans. Sometimes they have fish and chicken, but most families can afford meat on special occasions only. If you want to enjoy Roman food when you return to modern times back home, just ask—any good cook here will be glad to share a few recipes with you.

The poorest folks eat a lot of bread and a kind of cereal called *puls*. Those with a little money like to eat in the small taverns tucked into any street. Work your way through the crowds in the forum to one of the

FOODS TO TRY, at your own risk

Brain and Bacon Stew

Here's one recipe you might get from a local cook.

Ingredients
Head of a calf or pig
Hard-boiled eggs
Chicken giblets (the internal organs)
Cooked bacon
Black pepper and a few of your favorite herbs
A bit of wine
Flour and water

Directions
Remove the skin and nerves from the head. Scoop out the brains and boil them lightly. Strain the eggs with the brains. Chop up the chicken giblets, combine them with the eggs and brains, and mix it all together. Place the mixture into a pot. Crumble the bacon into the center of the eggs-and-brain mixture. Grind the pepper and sprinkle it over the mixture in the pot, along with the other herbs. Add a dash of wine and mix. Place the pot on an open fire and stir briskly with a whisk until the mixture is hot. Add flour and water and stir until the stew thickens. Enjoy!

many fast-food stands, called hot spots. A menu, sometimes written on a stone slab, will list sausages, chicken, ham, and bread. Eat in or take out. But be careful. There is no refrigeration, and food spoils quickly. Eat only freshly caught or preserved fish. The same advice goes for meats.

A Glass of Vinegar, Perhaps?

Wine is the most common drink for adults, but it is almost always diluted with water. Ordinary folks drink a very cheap wine called *posca*. Even after mixing it with water, it still tastes like vinegar.

Since you're traveling, you might be offered a honey refresher. This beverage is made by grinding pepper into a cup of honey and thinning it with a little water or wine. Romans drink it to renew energy and increase endurance.

Roman water that comes through a covered aqueduct is pretty clean. Nobody will think it's strange if you want to boil it, though. Many Romans drink a cup of hot water to start the day. If you can, get your drinking water from the highest point in the city. Some pipes drawing water into the city are lined with lead. Drinking water from lead pipes can cause physical and mental problems. Boiling the water doesn't help. To be really safe, ask a resident to keep you supplied with rainwater that's been collected for drinking.

A drinking glass from Pompeii

WHERE TO FIND SOUVENIRS

Roman jewelers produce exquisite cameos, but an elaborate cameo like this one will probably cost an awful lot.

STUFF YOU CAN CARRY

Romans think big, so many of their best creations aren't portable. Still, you can carry home lots of great things with you. While you're in the area of the forum, look for a bone-worker's shop, where you'll find attractive hair combs. Some are quite fancy. Or stop at a jeweler's and have a cameo made of your profile. Roman jewelers also make fine rings and pendants from amber. These jewelry artists can carve your initials in the amber and make you a personalized signet ring. A good way to remember the time you spent walking the streets of ancient Rome is to have a sandal maker create a pair of sandals measured just for you. You'll find the sandal makers all around the forum.

If you're in the Roman Empire in the first century A.D., Romans have mastered glassblowing techniques. You can find beautiful bottles and drinking glasses with designs etched or cut into the surface. Or you could bring back some easy-to-carry glass beads.

Rather have something that doesn't break? Coins are probably the easiest souvenirs to find and take with you. They're everywhere the Romans are. Depending on when you come to Rome, you can get coins made with images of the period's most popular emperors (such as Augustus or Trajan) or not-so-popular emperors (such as Nero or Domitian).

The emperor Titus had this brass sestersius minted for the grand opening of the Colosseum. It would make a great souvenir.

STUFF YOU CAN'T CARRY

You cannot take with you the beautiful public buildings, fountains, memorials, and triumphal arches you see in Rome. Still, you will see traces of these structures in modern buildings all around you when you get home.

Roman mosaics are striking in their colors and designs. Of course, you can't carry home a mosaic floor, either. But before you leave Rome, visit a mosaic shop. Watch the craftsmen plan out their design with tiles and glass. When you get home, you might want to try making your own souvenir with colorful squares of paper and some glue.

How to Stay Safe & Healthy

A pharmacist and her assistant prepare remedies.

Got a Snake Bite? Apply a Mouse!

The best doctors of the time are thought to be Greek. They are known for their rational approach to the causes and treatment of health problems. Romans tend to look to their gods and goddesses for help, often making offerings to ensure a good outcome when stricken with an illness. The goddess Febris is called upon to cure feverish diseases, for example. As Roman medicine advances, it becomes a blend of religious, folk, and scientific remedies and procedures.

Because of all their experience on the battlefields, Roman doctors are experts at treating wounds. First you clean the wound. Then you look around for an antiseptic (something to kill germs). Anything that stings will do. Wine, vinegar, and turpentine are Roman favorites. Or you can use a folk remedy, such as applying crushed cabbage to the injured area. Squashed earthworms, which are thought to boost the healing action, are also a popular cure. Snake bite? Rub the affected area with two halves of a mouse. If the wound is caused by something made from iron—such as an enemy's sword—pig manure may be the answer. Fresh is best, but powdered will do.

Roman army doctors have seen a lot of gangrene, a deadly condition that often infects wounds of the arms and legs. The treatment of choice? Lop off the affected limb. Amputations are common practice in the military hospitals scattered throughout the empire. Artificial limbs are available, but they are expensive.

Some surgeries are done routinely, such as the removal of small tumors. Certain eye conditions are also treated surgically, including cataracts. The Romans have excellent surgical instruments, such as scalpels, probes, and forceps. They also have a tool that is capable of cutting through the skull. This can be used for surgeries of the head, even the brain. Local doctors have some painkillers but no anesthetic that is sure to keep you unconscious long enough. So if you need a surgeon, get a speedy one.

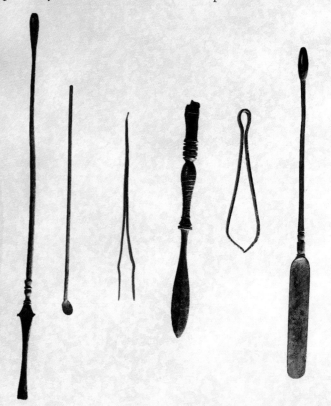

Some Roman surgical instruments look familiar in modern times, such as the forceps (third from left).

If you are visiting Rome as late as A.D. 162, the doctor you want is Galen. He comes to Rome from one of the empire's conquered cities and will become one of the most famous physicians in history. His years of treating gladiators have given him an insider's knowledge of the human body, as well as skill in surgery. His many books on anatomy and the scientific treatment of disease will influence the practice of medicine into the Middle Ages (A.D. 500–1500).

Or if you prefer, you could go to a woman doctor. Medicine is one of the few professions open to women in ancient Rome. Most women doctors are Greek, though, not Roman. There are also midwives, who specialize in assisting women during pregnancy and childbirth.

IMPORTANT
Safety Tip

Don't worry if you break a tooth. Roman dentists can cap teeth and even do bridgework (provide replacement teeth). They aren't too experienced with dental fillings, though. Romans don't get many cavities.

"BIRTHDAY FEVER" & OTHER COMPLAINTS

As the empire spreads to distant lands, new diseases pop up in Rome. Outbreaks of a deadly disease, possibly smallpox, occur between A.D. 164 and 189. Take special care to avoid Rome in A.D. 166, a year of devastating plague. Citizens try cleaning the air by burning bonfires. It doesn't help. Malaria is also a risk, so stay away from marshy areas.

One Roman author tells of a less serious ailment, known as Birthday Fever. The sufferer experiences a sudden rise in temperature until his or her birthday is over. If you get it and someone throws you a party, go. There will be lots of food, some presents, and maybe even a poem written just for you. The fever will run its course.

CRIME & PUNISHMENT

Although Rome's prefect—who's a sort of chief of police—has well-trained military troops as his policemen, crime is still a problem in the city. You have a good chance of being mugged if you go out after dark alone. But you can be robbed or assaulted at home, too. The best defense is to stay alert and, whenever possible, have a companion with you. Make lots of noise if a stranger approaches, especially at night.

Rome has a strong legal system, in case you do run into trouble. As early as 451 or 450 B.C., the first Roman laws were written down for all citizens to see. These laws, which were probably carved into wooden tablets, are known as the Laws of the Twelve Tables. Every male citizen was expected to know these rules by heart. Here are a few laws from the Twelve Tables:

- Whoever is in need of evidence, he shall go on every third day to shout before the witness's door.
- If a father surrenders his son for sale three times, the son shall be free from his father.
- If any person had sung or composed against another person a song such as was causing slander or insult to another, he should be clubbed to death.

You may find the Roman laws and penalties to be extreme. But the Romans saw the law as something to be interpreted and changed to fit the society and the times. Roman laws start out as generally agreed upon standards of right and wrong. But they can be adapted to the traditions and changing ideas of the people. This flexibility allows Rome to develop a single system of law that successfully governs the many different cultures of the empire.

Back TO THE FUTURE

The laws of many modern countries are based on the Roman legal system.

All Roman citizens have certain basic legal rights, including the right of due process. Due process means that laws must be stated clearly and carried out fairly. Citizens must be told what they've done wrong. They have the right to be tried by a jury, to defend themselves, and to appeal a court's decision and try to get it changed.

Such rights do not extend to slaves. Owners decide what is a crime and what isn't. They decide the punishment, too. But if you visit Rome around A.D. 50, you'll see that some laws are being made to protect slaves, as well—at least from the most brutal owners.

You'll find that Romans don't like the idea of prisons. When someone is declared guilty and sent to jail, it won't be for long. More direct action will be taken. Even though the law is supposed to be fair, that action will depend on the wealth and status of the accused person.

When the rich are found guilty of a serious crime, they're often forced to leave Rome. They kiss their property good-bye—and their citizenship. Then they usually go someplace sunny to live in relative comfort.

The poor, if convicted, face other possibilities—all bad. They lose the little property they might have, of course. After that they're beaten. If they are sentenced to death, they can be put in a sack and thrown in the Tiber River to drown. Some are burned alive, crucified, or thrown to the beasts at the Colosseum. And, of course, gladiator school is always an option.

FIRE, BAD EMPERORS, & OTHER DANGERS

Fire is the greatest danger you will face while visiting ancient Rome. Be on guard, especially if you're staying the night in a crowded neighborhood. The multistory buildings (some as high as six floors) are extreme fire hazards. The city fire brigades have to carry water to the fire in buckets filled at fountains or wells, which slows them down. The poor, who often live on the upper floors of tenements, have only a narrow staircase for an escape. Wealthy Romans who rent luxury apartments live on the ground floor and keep teams of slaves trained to put out fires in their homes.

Bad emperors can also be a problem. You might want to avoid Rome during the reigns of Caligula (A.D. 37–41) and Nero (A.D. 54–68). Caligula starts out okay, but then he begins to do strange things. He accuses people of treason and has them executed. He declares himself a god. Some say that he appoints his favorite horse to the Senate. Fearing what he might do next, members of his own military guard murder him to protect the empire.

Nero isn't much better. The Great Fire of A.D. 64, which destroys Rome's center, takes place during his reign. Many citizens believe that Nero himself set the fire. The fact that he builds a huge villa—so lavish that it was called the Golden House—on the site that was burned increases suspicion.

In addition to other shortcomings, Nero spends all the money in the treasury. He is so unpopular that Roman citizens openly rebel against him in A.D. 68. When he commits suicide, it causes a power struggle for the empire. As a result, during A.D. 69, Rome has four different emperors. It is a year of civil war, political intrigue, murder, and confusion.

TAKE IT from a Local

Nero's new home has an entry hall so big that he can place a 125-foot statue of himself there. Much of the house is overlaid with gold and decorated with gems. The main banquet hall revolves on a base. When the house is finished, it is said that Nero exclaims, "Ah! At last I can begin to live like a human being."

—*paraphrase of Suetonius's* Life of Nero

If you're still in Rome in A.D. 180, it's time to go home—soon! The emperor Commodus takes power in October. During his reign, he renames the empire, the Roman people, the Senate—even all the months of the year—after himself. He executes members of the Senate and seizes their wealth. Meanwhile, warring tribes threaten the empire's northern and eastern borders, and the Pax Romana comes to an end.

WHO'S WHO IN ANCIENT ROME

MARCUS AURELIUS (MARCUS AURELIUS ANTONINUS)

Marcus Aurelius (A.D. 121–180) is the last of the Five Good Emperors, a series of very competent rulers who oversee the final years (A.D. 96–180) of the Pax Romana. Marcus Aurelius's reign (A.D. 161–180) is successful but very difficult and includes a terrible plague and attacks from outsiders on the empire's northern and eastern borders. Marcus Aurelius spends most of the last ten years of his life on the battlefield defending Rome from these invaders. During this time, he writes a twelve-volume work on his thoughts and beliefs, *Meditations of Marcus Aurelius*. Because he is known as a fair and moral leader, many later emperors will change their names to include his. This is to persuade the people that they are good leaders, too—even if they aren't. Marcus Aurelius makes one big mistake—he chooses his son Commodus as his heir to the empire. Commodus is not good emperor material. In fact, he may be insane. After he is assassinated in A.D. 192, the empire embarks on a century of upheaval.

CLAUDIUS (TIBERIUS CLAUDIUS DRUSUS NERO GERMANICUS)

Claudius (ca. 10 B.C.–A.D. 54) serves as Rome's emperor from A.D. 41 to 54, appointed by the same military guards that killed his nephew Caligula. Because he has physical disabilities, such as a limp, partial paralysis, and speaking difficulties, including a stammer, many assume that Claudius is unfit physically and intellectually for the job. That assumption is wrong. He is an expert scholar and the author of many historical writings. During his reign, Claudius seeks good relations with the Senate, builds and repairs public facilities, and improves conditions for the military. He also adds provinces to the empire, including Britain (something that the mighty Julius Caesar tried—but failed—to do). Concerned that Roman law be practiced fairly, he often serves as a judge in the courts. But he does not watch carefully enough over the people around him. Many of those working in his government enrich themselves at the public's expense. And his wife is thought to have killed him by slipping poisonous mushrooms into his food.

CLEOPATRA

Roman generals seemed to have a weakness for Cleopatra (69–30 B.C.), the queen of Egypt. Both Julius Caesar and his favorite general, Marcus Antonius (also known as Marc Antony), fell in love with her. She was not regarded as exceptionally beautiful, but she was smart, witty, and shrewd. Cleopatra was a descendant of the Hellenistic (Greek) queens, who were known for their ambition and political skill. She was a big factor in the downfall of both Caesar and Antonius. Their downfalls, in turn, decided the political history of Rome. Caesar's assassins had feared, among other things, that Cleopatra and any children that she had with Caesar would gain power over Rome. Later, Rome's conservative senators were troubled by the fact that she had won Antonius's loyalty as well. After Octavian defeated Antonius and Cleopatra at the Battle of Actium in 31 B.C., he went on to conquer Egypt. Antonius and Cleopatra both committed suicide, and by 27 B.C., the Roman Senate has given Octavian (then known as Augustus) the power of an emperor.

The Vestal Virgins

Being a vestal virgin is one of the few career paths available to Roman women. These ladies tend the sacred flame in the temple of Vesta, the goddess of the hearth and home. To get the job of a vestal virgin, you must be a girl between the ages of six and ten, and you must pledge your devotion to the goddess for the next thirty years of your life. You cannot marry, never mind have a boyfriend, during your years in the temple. Once a year, the virgins throw a party for Vesta, and practically everyone in Rome comes. Since the bakers get the day off to celebrate, the virgins have to bake bread for everybody. These women give up a lot for the goddess. But by Roman standards, it's all worth it: some of the best seats at the Colosseum are reserved for the virgins. Oh, and there's one important drawback to the job that you should know about before you apply. If you get caught being in a romantic relationship, you'll be buried alive.

Virgil (Publius Vergilius Maro)

The Aeneid, an epic poem written by Virgil (70–19 B.C.), is thought to be the greatest literary work in Latin. It tells of Rome's beginnings and attempts to justify the empire's right to rule over other peoples. Virgil spends his last years writing *The Aeneid*, but he dies before he can finish. Even unfinished, *The Aeneid* is more than four hundred pages long! Romans really get into Virgil's work. Some even believe that you can tell the future by opening one of his books at random and choosing a line. That line will tell you what's going to happen. Writers such as Virgil are encouraged by Augustus, whose reign (27 B.C.–A.D. 14) is also known as the golden age of Latin literature.

PREPARING FOR THE TRIP

MAKE YOUR OWN BATH OIL

Romans didn't use soap in their baths. Instead they rubbed their skin with olive oil and used metal tools called strigils to scrape themselves clean. You can get that nice, oily (but clean) feeling, too, by using great-smelling bath oils that you make yourself. Make sure to use only non-toxic, mild herbs. Some good choices are rosemary, lavender, sage, cloves, or even mild pizza spices, such as oregano, basil, and marjoram. When the oil is ready, test a small amount on your skin to see that it soothes rather than irritates. Use the oil only on your skin. Do not drink it.

- Fill a small, clear glass jar about two-thirds full with a mild dried herb, such as rosemary. Pour in enough olive oil to fill the jar. Leave the jar in a sunny window for about two weeks.
- Pour oil through a strainer and set it aside. Throw away the used herbs and put a fresh batch into the jar. Add the strained oil. Top the jar off with fresh oil and leave it in a sunny place for two more weeks.
- Strain the oil and store it in a dark glass jar or bottle. Tie a ribbon around the container if you're giving it as a present.

Who needs soap, when you can get clean and smell like a pizza, too?

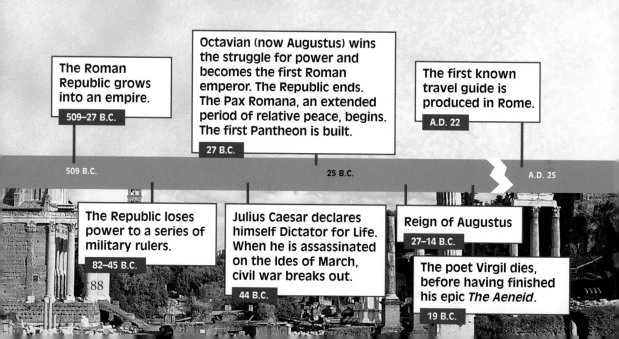

The Roman Republic grows into an empire.
509–27 B.C.

Octavian (now Augustus) wins the struggle for power and becomes the first Roman emperor. The Republic ends. The Pax Romana, an extended period of relative peace, begins. The first Pantheon is built.
27 B.C.

The first known travel guide is produced in Rome.
A.D. 22

509 B.C.

25 B.C.

A.D. 25

The Republic loses power to a series of military rulers.
82–45 B.C.

Julius Caesar declares himself Dictator for Life. When he is assassinated on the Ides of March, civil war breaks out.
44 B.C.

Reign of Augustus
27–14 B.C.

The poet Virgil dies, before having finished his epic *The Aeneid*.
19 B.C.

LEARN THE TRICKS OF THE TOGA

Think you'd look good in a toga? With some patience and a little help, you can find out.

- Get a bedsheet—the bigger, the better. (Oh, and you should probably ask someone first!) A typical queen-size flat sheet is 7 by 9 feet, and a king-size one is 9 by 9. Fold the sheet in half lengthwise.
- Put the folded sheet over your shoulders like a shawl. Pull one end over the front of your left shoulder so that it reaches your left ankle. Pull the other end under your right arm and across your chest to your left shoulder.
- Fasten the toga with a pin at the shoulder. Or, do what most Romans did: hold the toga up with your left hand, or pass it over your left shoulder and press down your arm to hold the toga against your side.
- If you have more length to play with, pass the toga over the left shoulder rather than pinning or holding it. Then pass it across your back and over the right shoulder. The more cloth you have, the better folds and drapes you'll get. These folds and drapes are not only stylish, they're useful. You can make them work as pockets, or even as a hood.
  Now try to walk and hold up your toga at the same time. If you can, you have the makings of a Roman citizen.

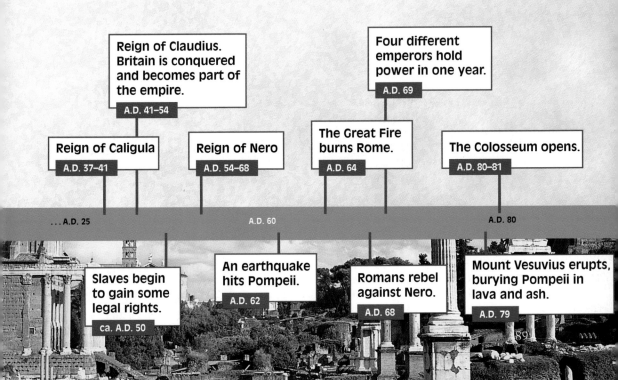

Reign of Claudius. Britain is conquered and becomes part of the empire.
A.D. 41–54

Four different emperors hold power in one year.
A.D. 69

Reign of Caligula
A.D. 37–41

Reign of Nero
A.D. 54–68

The Great Fire burns Rome.
A.D. 64

The Colosseum opens.
A.D. 80–81

. . . A.D. 25

A.D. 60

A.D. 80

Slaves begin to gain some legal rights.
ca. A.D. 50

An earthquake hits Pompeii.
A.D. 62

Romans rebel against Nero.
A.D. 68

Mount Vesuvius erupts, burying Pompeii in lava and ash.
A.D. 79

GLOSSARY

amphitheater: a large, usually oval, outdoor theater, with seats on all sides that are tiered to give the audience a clear view of the event

aqueduct: a structure that encloses a network of pipes carrying water from one point to another

artifact: an object of historical interest made by people

bust: a sculpture of a person's head

cataract: a clouding of the lens of the eye

dictator: a ruler who has total control over a government

dig: a site where archaeologists search for clues about earlier civilizations. Digs are also called excavations.

empire: a large, unified area that is controlled by one all-powerful ruler called an emperor

epic poem: a long poem that tells the history and legend of a people

fresco: a painting done directly on a wall's wet plaster

Middle East: a group of countries, ranging from North Africa to southwestern Asia, including Egypt, Israel, Turkey, and Iran

mime: a silent performance

mosaic: a design made from small squares of tile or glass that are cemented in place

province: outlying regions of a country or empire

republic: a country whose citizens elect individuals to govern for them

tenement: an apartment building, characterized by bad maintenance and crowded, possibly unsafe conditions

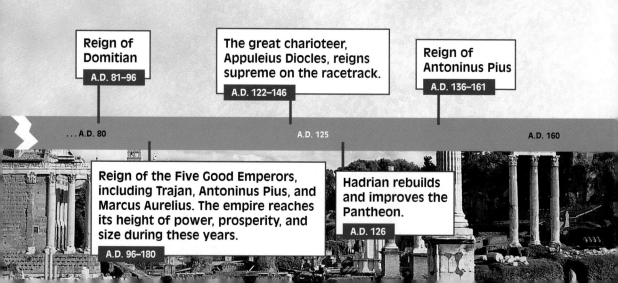

Reign of Domitian
A.D. 81–96

The great charioteer, Appuleius Diocles, reigns supreme on the racetrack.
A.D. 122–146

Reign of Antoninus Pius
A.D. 136–161

...A.D. 80   A.D. 125   A.D. 160

Reign of the Five Good Emperors, including Trajan, Antoninus Pius, and Marcus Aurelius. The empire reaches its height of power, prosperity, and size during these years.
A.D. 96–180

Hadrian rebuilds and improves the Pantheon.
A.D. 126

PRONUNCIATION GUIDE

Augustus	aw-GUHS-tuhs
aureus	OR-ee-uhs
Caligula	kuh-LIHG-yoo-luh
centuria	sehn-CHOOR-ee-uh
denarius	dih-NARE-ee-uhs
frigidarium	frihd-jih-DARE-ee-um
gnomon	NOH-muhn
Ides	EYEDZ
Kalends	KAL-uhnds
mare nostrum	MAHR-ay NAW-struhm
Nero	NEER-oh
Nones	NOHNZ
oculus	AWK-yoo-luhs
Pax Romana	PAHX roh-MAHN-uh
plebeians	pluh-BEE-uhns
Pompeii	pahm-PAY
sestertius	seh-STUR-shee-uhs
strigil	STRIH-juhl
Vesuvius	vih-SOO-vee-uhs

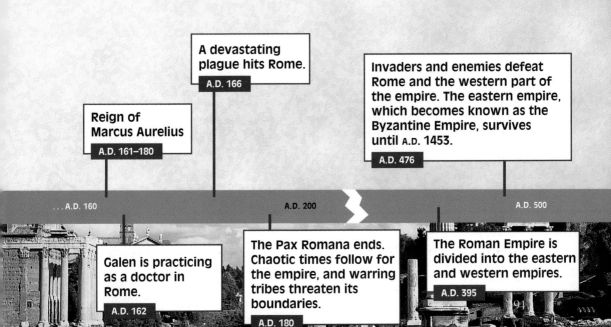

A devastating plague hits Rome.
A.D. 166

Invaders and enemies defeat Rome and the western part of the empire. The eastern empire, which becomes known as the Byzantine Empire, survives until A.D. 1453.
A.D. 476

Reign of Marcus Aurelius
A.D. 161–180

...A.D. 160   A.D. 200   A.D. 500

Galen is practicing as a doctor in Rome.
A.D. 162

The Pax Romana ends. Chaotic times follow for the empire, and warring tribes threaten its boundaries.
A.D. 180

The Roman Empire is divided into the eastern and western empires.
A.D. 395

91

FURTHER READING

Books

Barghusen, Joan. *Daily Life in Ancient and Modern Rome*. Minneapolis, MN: Runestone Press, 1999.

Behnke, Alison. *Italy in Pictures*. Minneapolis, MN: Lerner Publications Company, 2003.

DuTemple, Lesley A. *The Colosseum*. Minneapolis, MN: Lerner Publications Company, 2003.

———. *The Pantheon*. Minneapolis, MN: Lerner Publications Company, 2003.

Ganeri, Anita. *Emperors and Gladiators*. Chicago: Peter Bedrick Books, 2001.

Greenblatt, Miriam. *Augustus and Imperial Rome*. Tarrytown, NY: Benchmark Books, 2000.

Harris, Nicholas, and Peter Dennis (illustrator). *Volcano*. Hauppauge, NY: Barron's, 2001.

Haywood, John. *The Romans*. New York: Oxford University Press, 1996.

Langley, Andrew, and Philip DeSouza. *The Roman News*. Milwaukee: Gareth Stevens, 2000.

MacDonald, Fiona. *Women in Ancient Rome*. Lincolnwood, IL: Peter Bedrick Books, 2000.

McNeill, Sarah. *Ancient Romans at a Glance*. New York: Peter Bedrick Books, 1998.

Nardo, Don. *Games of Ancient Rome*. San Diego: Lucent Books, 2000.

Sheehan, Sean. *Ancient Rome*. Austin, TX: Raintree-Steck Vaughn, 2000.

Solway, Andrew, and Stephen Biesty. *Rome: In Spectacular Cross Section*. New York: Scholastic, 2003.

Woods, Michael and Mary B. Woods. *Ancient Construction: From Tents to Towers*. Minneapolis, MN: Runestone Press, 2000.

———. *Ancient Medicine: From Sorcery to Surgery*. Minneapolis, MN: Runestone Press, 1999.

Internet Sites

Ancient World Web
<http://www.julen.net/ancient/index.html>

BBC: The Romans
<http://www.bbc.co.uk/education/romans>

Historyforkids: Ancient Rome
<http://www.historyforkids.org/learn/romans/>

In Italy Online: Ostia Antica
<http://www.initaly.com/regions/latium/ostia.htm>

PBS: The Roman Empire in the First Century
<http://www.pbs.org/empires/romans/empire/index.html>

Political Offices in the Roman Republic
<http://www.vroma.org/~bmcmanus/romangvt.html>

Virtual Field Trip to Vesuvius
<http://www.brookes.ac.uk/geology/8361/2000/angela/home.htm>

BIBLIOGRAPHY

Adkins, Lesley, and Roy A. Adkins. *Handbook to Life in Ancient Rome*. New York: Oxford University Press, 1998.

British Columbia Library Association. *Ancient Rome Toga Time*. N.d. <http://www.bcpl.gov.bc.ca/src/2000/rome.html> (January 2002).

Byers, Doris. *Natural Body Basics: Making Your Own Cosmetics*. Bargerville, IN: Gooseberry Hill Publications, 1996.

Camden, David. *Forum Romanum*. 2003. <http://www.forumromanum.org> (July 2003).

Cartwright, Frederick F. *Disease and History*. New York: Dorset Press, 1972.

Compact World Atlas. New York: Dorling Kindersley Publishing, 2001.

Davison, Michael Worth, ed. *Everyday Life through the Ages*. London: Reader's Digest, 1992.

De Souza, Philip. "Ancient Rome and the Pirates." *History Today,* July 2001, 48–54.

Dunkel, Roger. "A Day in the Life of an Ancient Roman." N.d. <http://depthome.brooklyn.cuny.edu/classics/dunkle/romnlife/index.htm> (July 2003)

Freeman, Charles. *Greece and Rome: Civilizations of the Ancient Mediterranean*. New York: Oxford University Press, 1996.

Grant, Michael. *A Social History of Greece and Rome*. New York: Charles Scribner's Sons, 1992.

Gruen, Erich S. "Ancient Rome." *World Book Encyclopedia*. Vol. 16. Chicago: World Book, Inc., 1992.

Lefkowitz, Mary R., and Maureen B. Fant. "The Law of the Twelve Tables." *Women's Life in Greece and Rome*. N.d. <http://www.uky.edu/ArtsSciences/Classics/wlgr/wlgr-romanlegal.html> (March 2002).

Majno, Guido. *The Healing Hand: Man and Wound in the Ancient World*. Cambridge, MA: Harvard University Press, 1991.

Matz, David. *Daily Life of the Ancient Romans*. Westport, CT: Greenwood Press, 2001.

Payne, Robert, et al. *The Horizon Book of Ancient Rome*. New York: American Heritage Publishing Co., 1966.

Ryan, Tim. "Julio-Claudians 27 B.C.–68 A.D." *Dead Romans, The Emperors Site*. N.d. <http://home.nyc.rr.com/deadromans/romanemp/#Julio-Claudians> (March 2002).

Scarre, Chris. *The Penguin Historical Atlas of Ancient Rome*. New York: Penguin Putnam, Inc., 1995.

Stone, Judith. "Thumb and Thumber." *Discover,* December 1996, 62–64.

Time-Life editors. *What Life Was Like When Rome Ruled the World*. Alexandria, VA: Time-Life, Inc., 1997.

INDEX

Rita J. Markel's stories and historical articles for children and teens have appeared in both magazines and books (some under her pseudonym, Bonnie Brightman). She is also the author of a young adult biography of rock legend Jimi Hendrix. A former teacher, she lives in Idaho with her husband and son.

Acknowledgments for Quoted Material p. 22, as quoted by Michael Worth Davison, ed., *Everyday Life through the Ages* (London: Reader's Digest, 1992); p. 34, as quoted by Guido Majno, *The Healing Hand: Man and Wound in the Ancient World* (Cambridge, MA: Harvard University Press, 1991); p. 55 as quoted by Robert Payne et al., *The Horizon Book of Ancient Rome* (New York: American Heritage Publishing Co., 1966); p. 63, as quoted by Time-Life editors, *What Life Was Like When Rome Ruled the World* (Alexandria, VA: Time-Life, Inc., 1997); p. 84, as quoted by David Matz, *Daily Life of the Ancient Romans* (Westport, CT: Greenwood Press, 2001).

Photo Acknowledgments The images in this book are used with the permission of: © Scott Gilchrist/Archivision Inc., pp. 2, 6–7, 38, 56, 70, 73; © Historical Picture Archive/CORBIS, p. 11; © The Art Archive/Bibliothèque des Arts Décoratifs Paris/Dagli Orti, p. 13; © The Art Archive/Museo della Civilta Romana Rome/Dagli Orti, pp. 15, 40, 44 (top), 50, 87; © The Art Archive/The Art Archive, p. 17; © Van der Heyden Collection/IPS, pp. 19, 28, 36, 62, 65, 72, 88, 89, 90, 91; © Erich Lessing/Art Resource, NY, pp. 20, 43, 46; © Roger Ressmeyer/CORBIS, p. 23; © Araldo de Luca/CORBIS, pp. 24, 52, 54, 79; © Bettmann/CORBIS, pp. 26, 69; Library of Congress, pp. 2 (LC-USZ62-97804), 35 (LC-USZ62-97803), 39 (LC-USZ62-115366), 41 (LC-USZ62-084594), 57 (LC-USZ62-101210), 85 (LC-USZ62-120252); © Sandro Vannini/CORBIS, p. 29; © North Wind Picture Archives, p. 30; © Scala/Art Resource, NY, p. 32; © Copyright The British Museum, p. 44 (bottom), 78; © The Art Archive/Archaeological Museum Beirut/Dagli Orti, p. 45; © The Art Archive/Museo Prenestino Palestrina, p. 47; © Angelo Hornak/CORBIS, p. 48; © The Art Archive/Archaeological Museum Naples/Dagli Orti, pp. 55, 74; © Hulton Archive by Getty Images, p. 58; © Borromeo/Art Resource, NY, p. 60; © Mimmo Jodice/CORBIS, p. 63; © Roger Wood/CORBIS, pp. 66–67, 71, 86; © The Art Archive/Harper Collins Publishers, p. 76; © The Art Archive/Bibliothèque Nationale Paris/The Art Archive, p. 77; © The Art Archive/Archaeological Museum Châtillon-sur-Seine/Dagli Orti, p. 80; maps and illustration pp. 8–9, 14 by Laura Westlund; cartoons by Tim Parlin.

Front Cover: The Art Archive/Musée du Louvre Paris/Dagli Orti (top), The Art Archive/Archaeological Museum Naples/Dagli Orti (bottom)